ANTHOLOGY FOR

Hope

IN THE

*H*OOD

Jess Marie

ANTHOLOGY FOR HOPE IN THE HOOD

Copyright 2015 By Jessica Marie Smith

PUBLISHED BY

Jessica Marie Smith

P.O. Box 7113

Novi, MI 48376

Email: jsmithcoinc@gmail.com

Book cover and page design by Shannon Crowley,

Treasure Image & Publishing - TreasureImagePublishing.com

Edited by

Wanda J. Burnside

Write the Vision Ministries and Media Productions Int'l -

thecalledandreadywriters.org

and

Minister Mary D. Edwards,

Leaves of Gold Consulting, LLC - LeavesOfGoldConsulting.com

CONTENTS

ACKNOWLEDGEMENTS

I want to personally thank my editor, Wanda J. Burnside for all of the time, patience and effort that went into producing my book. Every one of her reminders to keep writing and to believe that this could be accomplished is the very reason this book was able to be written. A very sincere thank you to Mrs. Wanda Burnside; without your believing I could do this, I would only be wishing I could.

To all of the members of The Called and Ready Writers Guild, I thank each of you all for your encouragement and examples. I am also eternally grateful for the vision and prayers of Founder Minister Mary D. Edwards concerning this work. It is such a treasure to be considered a part of this organization.

I appreciate my church family at Trinity Deliverance Church, my Pastor, Apostle Diane Washington, who saw me as a writer, pushed me toward my dream of writing and has led by example in living purposefully. I am also eternally grateful to the following individuals who have made significant contributions as spiritual teachers and examples: Pastor Joseph Stevenson, Pastor Maurice Stimage, Elder Michael Fields and Elder Sean Holland.

I am grateful for all of my family, friends, spiritual family, and co-workers who listened to my poems read from a tattered notebook. Thank you for your patience, for listening and allowing me to be excited and passionate about writing.

TO GOD BE THE GLORY!

INTRODUCTION

"*Anthology for Hope in the Hood,*" is a collection of poetry to inspire those who look for hope amidst seemingly hopeless circumstances. The "*Hope in the Hood*" theme is an aim to reach the young, the experienced, the churched and the unchurched. True hope is what gives humanity purpose.

Often times, our environment predetermines our hope. Real hope, however, is not determined by our predicaments. It can only be found in Christ. This collection of poems gives a practical, understandable, and enjoyable demonstration of things hoped for. This is an anthology for hope in the hood.

PREFACE

"*Anthology for Hope in the Hood: Book One*" is the first book of a three part series. It is to encourage people of faith and to minister to anyone struggling with issues that surround "the hood." The poems present practical issues that many face alone. There were times where I hoped to get away from "the hood" as I grew up in Detroit. Hope resonated in both the good and bad times. A hope to make a better life, to escape some of the painful snares and generational bondages our elders may have fallen into. The "hood" is not just a place of despair, but of community and the place where many people like me were developed. The "hood" is where we need to sow seeds of hope, as it is so much a part of our roots.

In the *Anthology for Hope in the Hood* series, poetic lyrics are used to bring the reader into a visualization of the everyday realities that come with urban living. Some of the stigma surrounding the inner-city life and situations we may face are not only particular to the ghettos across the land. Hope is not just for those without it. Hope is for all. We all hope for the best... and somehow we get through.

The focus on the 'hood is not excluding those who may not live in the city. Because true hope is founded in faith; those without faith, without love and without God, also need to be introduced to the *Anthology for Hope in the Hood*. As you read, you will travel through issues of alcoholism, abuse, depression, and hopelessness. Please consider what you hope for now and eternally.

EDITOR COMMENTARY

POET JESSICA SMITH: A Voice like a Trumpet

"Cry aloud, spare not; Lift up your voice like a trumpet; Tell My People their transgression, And the house of Jacob their sins" (Isaiah 58:1 NKJV).

Author Jessica Smith is a bold, courageous, and prolific poet. She is full of wisdom beyond her years. Jessica is perceptive and keenly knowledgeable about the struggles, devastation, and pitfalls in our society. She is sensitive to the deception of Satan to mark the mind, the emotions, and soul with evil thoughts which lead to tormenting agony in the depths of the soul.

She is like the fearless, forthright, outspoken, and frank ancient Biblical prophets who God used like Elisha, Elijah, Isaiah, Samuel, and others to proclaim the Word of God. Through her edgy and razor-sharp written words, she declares truths to reflect the mighty Word of God in critical situations, trials, and challenges in life. Today, there are crucial and serious issues to confront from the range of sexual relationships to abusive living from drugs and crime, to all manner of sin. Jessica addresses them from her heart. She speaks to the church to be committed and responsible to what is godly and spiritually required of them.

Jessica's poetry is soulful and daring, like the masterful African-American poets: Langston Hughes, Gwendolyn Brooks, Nikki

Giovanni, Maya Angelou, and other greats. She brings a depth of poetry that goes below the surface of difficulties, challenges, and false excuses. Jessica uncovers the lies, misconceptions, and phony dealings in deceitful hearts.

In this book, you will be confronted with truth and reality. She makes sure that you clearly understand that there are broken, hurting, sinful, and deprived people living among us. She intensely speaks to your heart and intellect to awaken them from sleep and to face what is real and true. Jessica firmly stands knowing and believing that the only answer to our sinful sick society and brokenness is Jesus Christ our Lord and Savior!

Mrs. Wanda J. Burnside, Poetry Editor and President
The Called and Ready Writers

Circle of Influence

Without rhyme or reason,
It seems like treason,
When so-called saints
Stop believing.
Words confounding,
To start deceiving.

I hope people recognize
Encamped about by angels,
There are devils in disguise
Very rarely transformed
By the renewing of the mind
A circle of influence,
The storm is coming.

Dark days, close in all around me
Hope prays,
A voice deep inside me.

But I do not hear it.
I do not know how to listen.
Too blinded by diamonds,
As they shine and glisten.

Drawn in by desire,
I do not know it's tight.
Lusting after power,
I do not care what's right.

A circle of influence,
That pays most well,
As I sit and watch
From a beautiful hell.

With friends that smile
Like a Cheshire cat.
As they disappear,
Who needs enemies,
To turn their back?

Friends are disappointed.
When you don't do
What they want.
They are not my idols.
But in my quest to change my ways,
And desire not,
They have become my rivals.

Where can I run to?
When I am standing in despair?
I pray some god can hear me,
From way over there.

A circle of influence changing,
For there has been a shifting.
Heavy burden disengaging,
Under heavy sifting
Made confession once before,
But behold,
Yet a new thing.
Delivered, go, and sin no more,
In the presence of a true King.

The cycles are now breaking.
I thought they never would!
I see these days as evil
And only God as good.

I talk to old friends,
They think that I am strange.
I say I am following God,
They say I am deranged.

But there is no denying,
I have truly changed.
The circle of influence dismantled,
Now free from bond and chain.

I continue to pray for my friends,
As they murmur idle words.
I pray the Spirit speak to them,
Confirming what was heard.

As they speak,
I pray and smile…
Knowing it may take a while.

May the knowledge of God
Dwell in them richly,
May salvation come to them,
And may it happen quickly.

The Spirit is speaking clearly,
And time is running out:
Chose ye therefore this day,
What you will be about.

Some circle at the outer courts,
While I am going in,
Longing for God's righteousness
And fellowship with them.
The blessing of the Lord has no sorrow.
I choose to follow Him.
No more wrestling for joy tomorrow,
I have His peace within.

Those friends are far away from me,
But the Lord is my treasure
Following willingly,
As God's light and truths
Make me better.

I chose to leave the pack,
My circle of influence.
For their lifestyle is wack,
They don't know what they're doing!

I am secure in the Lord,
Resting in His hand.
Only serving Him,
On His Word I stand.
Psalm 1:1

Looking to Heaven in Grayscale

Dark past,
Black heart.
Wanting hope,
Faith no part.
Looking to the sky,
No light shining,
Grayscale is why.

Look above to see the clouds
Heaven's light breaks,
Though darkness crowds.
Looking to Heaven in Grayscale.

What shapes a limited perspective?
Limited resources with infinite blessing
No Son-light coming in,
Everything around looks grim.

Looking to Heaven in Grayscale.
Somehow beautiful,
From a miserable hell,

Looking up,
Though dimly sought.
Standing strong,
Though daily fought.
The city of Heaven
In the thickest cloud,
Running the race,
Before the witnessing crowd.

Worldview

Don't nobody tell me what to think,
I'm grown!
You can't say my ship will sink,
I'm on my own!
How can you say that I will fail?
Who do you think you are to tell?

Views of the world,
Opinions and thoughts,
Paying dues for the life we bought.
Anybody tells to do what ought,
Yet we have given all for naught.

He said. They said.
Not much said.

Following the system,
Without much led,
About that life,
The one that's dead.
Why can't these people,
Get it in they head?

They say it's OK!
To have an abortion.
That if you deny you're gay,
Life is torture.
Why is sin part of church culture?
Got a mixed bag,
With a small Jesus portion.

Oh we clap our hands,
Inside God's house.
And we say "Amen"
As we dance and shout.

Yet, our feet never move
To walk it out,
Believing for Blessing,
Though Salvation we doubt.

What has caused this infiltration?
Are we not a Holy nation?
Have we forgotten our motivation,
That we now turn to masturbation?

The World says everything is okay,
And that God will love you anyway.
They deny a literal hell. MAYDAY!
But trust the Lord, come what may.

Church!!
We're too concerned about what they say.
The world stepped in
And choked our faith.
But to spiritual death, nay.
God grant us mercy, we pray.

What is shaping your opinion?
Are you too bewildered,
To give up sinning?
How about a start with some repenting?
Then God can address
How you should be living.

Don't worry about
Being a narrow-minded Christian.
Hear God's voice and listen.
His Word and Spirit quicken,
To shift a Worldly Christian.

Examining Hope

Dime on the Floor

I looked down and saw a dime on the floor,
I see myself as worth much more.
How did a piece that shines
Land in this place,
As wasted value,
And talent misplaced?

I wonder who left the dime behind.
Will they see my change in time?
Something so small
Can make a difference,
When constantly short-changed
By any ignorance.

I see a dime on the floor,
Myself, and my value worth much more.
I pick it up,
Place it in my purse,
To remind me of
My never-changing worth.

Spirits

I see a sign for "food and spirits,"
I stop in for grease and chicken.
Needing something to wash it down,
Started light now about to clown.

Got a few in me,
So I'm feeling myself.
My life tastes rich,
So I'm going top shelf.

No worries about being hung-over.
No concern about
My morrow's pungent odor.
I have perfume for that.

Look like I have my bases covered,
But no notion of the spirits hovered.
Only feels good when I can get a drink,
But never did I stop to think....
What drives me this way?

Thought I had it figured out,
Though my mind
Now is filled with doubt.
I need a drink so I can think.
There, a woman in pretty pink.
I see a man on the brink.

I think to myself,
What a sloppy drunk.
As I walk over him,
He really stunk.
He can't hold his liquor,
While I am drinking quicker.

I sink into a fairy land,
Where the world is in my hand.
All around me, watching eyes,
As they tell their varied lies.
But no surprise there!
What do I care,
I'm drunk.

Enjoying the moment–
And about to put a ring up on it.
Drinking peace for the turmoil within,
Filled with spirit, though full of sin.
The wrong spirits have gotten in,
And from the glass I cannot win

I'm defeated,
As I lay on the sidewalk.
I'm dead,
Line me with chalk.
I'm too drunk to even talk.
But the Angel of the Lord stepped in,
And lifted my head once again.

By the Spirit of God I raised,
By God's mercy I was saved.
The spirit of alcoholism
Left with utter haste.
Now, I am living free by God's grace.

Fielding Dreams

Across the street is an empty field,
A field of dreams.
Dreams deferred,
Success deterred.
Dandelions wave in the sun,
Looking like beauty more than a weed.
No hope in my neighborhood, just bushes.

Vicious cycles are on the block,
But I see nice cars.
No one believes in anything –
Because they pray,
And nothing changed,
With God.

I just sit on the porch most days.
And run inside when I hear shots.
Kids have a lot of energy.
They must be fools.
Nothing more fun than
When we dress as ghouls.

Day to day,
It's dark under the sun.
Hope lies and dreams kill.
I check my pulse
Because I'm breathing still.

I got to make some choices,
So I get off the porch.
I say a quick prayer,
I light up my torch.

Making my way through the darkness,
Pass the empty field of dreams,
Past; the empty dreams I'm fielding.

Beginning to believe,
Opening eyes to see,
Hearing a voice
Though I am feeling schizophrenic;
Changing my surroundings,
Though I am still living in it.

Hoping, praying
Now expected,
A God-representation,
Now elected,
Expelling the principles
Of natural selection.

Money is no longer going for gold.
Not listening to fortunes told.
Because of Christ, I am fearless and bold.
Awakening to glory, a sight to behold.

Transformed by a renewed mind,
Living for sights of glory divine,
Neighbors see me now–
And they think I'm flexing.
They think I have money now,
Because my joy's perplexing.

But, I am thanking my God
Though it might seem odd,
The hell I had to face,
I ain't forgot!

Empty fields now under my feet –
No more weights,
I can't be beat!

I have faith,
Feeling awake and alive.
Dreams are becoming a reality.
Trusting in God that I will survive,
Of hopelessness, no longer a casualty.

Behind me now is,
An empty field of dreams
With faith in action,
The challenge is not what it seems.

Suicide Doors

Suicide doors pull up
To neighborhood stores.
Looking out the window,
While mopping the kitchen floor.

Day to day life is easy,
Though each moment
Is nothing pleasing.

Windows circle about suicide doors,
While gold-rimmed glasses
Highlight black tints.
Looks good on first glance,
Second look, a bit more tense.

The driver with a hand in the lap,
Holding the trigger of a forty-five,
Not too trigger-happy,
With nothing for to stay alive.

Pain inside suicide doors
That lift up to the sky.
Hearts fall on floorboards,
When men try to die.

There are no hands praying,
As they open suicide doors.

Watcher in the window,
Standing on a chair
Suicide doors open
To watcher in despair.
Not too long before watching eyes
Fall into a stare.

Suicide doors swing in the wind,
It seems like no hope is getting in.
Just despair as the end of things begin,
Feel the moment coming in.

Torment, anger, shame, defeat
A strongman rising, hard to seat.
Demons crowding,
Feeling hungry.
Darkness coming,
All surrounding.

Cannot breathe,
Close the door.
Suicide, death,
Wanting more…
"Resist and it will flee,"
Says the Voice of Victory.

Tears well up inside of eyes,
As thoughts begin to stabilize.
Hope alive stands outside
As suicide doors cannot be pried,
A moment for death drawing nigh.

Then a flash –
Suicide doors drawing back.
Angels that one cannot see
Save a life from death by rescuing.

Left, a broken rope that cannot choke.
A smoking gun, just a puff of smoke.
A flash of glory for hopeless eyes,
Death interrupted by angels in disguise.

A knock on the window of suicide doors.
A doorbell heard from kitchen floors.
Life is given back.

Suicide doors now shut closed.
Peace, joy, and life now transposed.
For the aid of a lonely soul,
The breath of God proved instrumental.
In the closing of doors more incidental,
Than their place on Lincoln's Continental.

LOOKING FOR HOPE

Street Song

Going to the church with my street song.
Giving all I got 'til I go home.
After a few hours,
Then I am back on.
With a song on repeat,
How we sing along.

More than a gospel rap
And a sly foot tap.
A little more than a free rat
Outside a mousetrap.
Okay, my waved hands
And my church clap.
Oh how that music
Does take me back.

Hum along with the street song.
Counting every fleeting moment dung.
Waiting for my come along.
Tired of this ratchet street song.
The wheels go round
While the bus trots along.

These streets could not save me,
They take everything they gave me,
I take what I got on the street.
To feed what I need to eat.
On the streets they demand loyalty.
When the music stops, all I got is me.

Ain't no love in the streets.
My heart is a heavy drum beat.
I thank my God,
Jesus saved me.
Now I go preaching in the streets,
And the angels sing when I speak.

Blue and Black Girl

Blue and Black Girl,
With Hair full of Curl.
Alone in a Cold World,
Trying to find a Straight head.

Trying to love the truth,
Sleeping with a lie
Thinking what's the use,
Why even try
Little blue girl,
Little black girl
Looking for peace
From an evil world.

The concept of hope becomes absurd,
When the search ends,
All stones unturned.

Looking out the window,
With a fist clinched,
Releasing a banded arm,
With a vein pinched.

No hope for loss souls.
No escape as rain pours.
No pain in black and blue arms.
No bruises mean no harms.

Blue and black girl
Wanting beauty in an ugly world
No kind words to be heard,
Just broken ribs and hummingbirds.

Working black girl—
Alone in a white world
Blue days unfurled
While nervous, short locks twirled.

Little blue and black girl,
Came to church after last night's cry
Greetings from the people
In their own world
Too busy to notice
The handprint on her eye.

No peace, no rest.
But somehow she stays blessed,
Healing comes with sweet rest,
While living with no death.

Peace abide,
Deep inside.
Blue and black,
Now no lack.

Blue and black girl
Once alone in the world,
Now has release
From the God of Peace
No abuse or rejection by resurrection
What was blackened coal,
Is now diamond and gold.
Value added to a once wretched soul.

From The Hood Came Ain't

Mama said, "You ain't got."
Daddy said, "You ain't going."
Teacher said, "You ain't smart."
Preacher said, "You ain't growing."
Friends said, "I ain't changed."

Everybody tell me what I ain't.
I can't even see my reflection.
All around me, I hear I can't,
I need a new direction.

I need somebody to speak to me
And tell me that I CAN.
I need a hand to reach for me
And help my soul to stand.

Ain't you tired of hearing
What you ain't?
And WHY you trying,
When you can't?

Positivity is hard to find,
When you fighting against yo own mind.
But have hope, and have heart,
Don't let this world tear you apart.

I hope they hear
And don't say they ain't.
Reach for the hope that's near,
And don't say you can't.

From the hood came ain't
And it has been a struggle.
Fear will tell me I can't,
And the devil brings me trouble.

But I was taught to fear God,
And trust the Shepherd's rod.

STOP hearing **ain't!**
Quit listening at **can't!**

Most folks know we can do
All things through Christ
But do you know you can
Really live this life?
A life in God's will,
A life in His hand.
Change your will to,
Through Christ I can.

Gotta Be Something More

It's gotta be something more
For these girls to do,
Than working at a strip club.
They look to lies and false true,
Clinging to false love.

A pile of money,
But a life in shambles.
No sweet for Honey,
As a corner preacher rambles.

Words of life,
Fall on ears of the dead.
Days full of strife,
As the people are misled.

A liquor store on the corner,
A church on the block.
A strip joint as they sojourner,
While pulling out a glock.

I live "Breaking News" every day,
Hoping the pain will go away.
But, I go home and lock the door,
Only to go at it again once more.

Scratches on the outside,
Trying to get in
Shaking myself,
Though my fate looks grim
I gotta get away!
Looking for a brighter day.

Life is the raw and the natural,
Yet, I consume and chew
Artificial moments.
Hoping to expel happiness,
Only to regurgitate emptiness.

Somebody on the corner yelling "Jesus!"
I open up a window.
We all need somebody to lead us.
I never trusted Him, so…

Guess I gotta try,
Before I die.
Which could be any day,
If I continue this way.
It's gotta be something more,
See what salvation has in store.

IN THE HOOD

Stay the Course

The race is not given to the swift,
And the money don't last that long.
The war is not won by arms,
And our fervor ain't so strong.

Stay the course 'til you get home.
Be encouraged, it won't be too long.

Praying God keeps you safe.
Prayers uttered in total faith.
Be of good cheer, my dearest dear,
May the Lord Jesus keep you near.
May God extend to you His grace,
May His glory shine upon your face.

Whether in class or on the street,
May the Lord God ever guide your feet.
May your joys be ever new,
While your faith in God ever true.

Stay the Course!
This is not a thought or suggestion,
More a demand and instruction.
Please, please remain focused I plead,
As the Lord fulfills your every need.

A lot may come day to day,
But stay the course come what may.
Hold ever true to salvation,
Remain unmoved, without reservation.

Until the final stretch, fight for flight
Toward the goal,
Press with all your strength and might.

Be glad dear youth!
Pursue good and truth!

Stay the course 'til you get home.
Be encouraged, it won't be too long.

Faith Life

It takes faith to live in the hood
How could I be an atheist?
Even when things don't look good,
Somehow we still making it.

Bills come harder than bullets.
Darkest of nights, we get through it.
We rise like the Son,
Through whom all is won.
Yet, is not the day done.

In moments of despair,
While we gasping for air,
We lift our hands high,
And reach for the sky.

While we are beat down
And moments fly by,
We are not shot down
By the attempt of a drive by.
In assassination of our dreams,
To hope in Christ Jesus we cling.

When all seems lost,
He paid the cost.

It takes faith to live in the hood,
Even when things don't look so good.
When the purpose of life is misunderstood,
I can still look to the hood.
Time with the fam, sitting in the shade
Sitting on the porch, like we got it made.

There is a rest only found in God
Not in money or cars
Trusting in God is my daily bread
Rather than living hood,
I'm living faith instead.

How Else Can I Relate

How else can I relate?
Why not make them anticipate?
It's rough out here with these guys,
Everyday ain't hard though,
I embellish lies.

In my lyrics,
I'm too near it.
But on the real,
No deal.

Rappers out here be lying,
Saying they gone be rich or die trying.
Fact of the matter,
They lose they head like the mad hatter.

Putting hope in faithless things,
Boosted up by mindless youth
Because of a name.

You don't like conscious music?
Open your mouth and put something to it.
Maybe some thought once in a while,
Otherwise be a silly child.

Set some goals to accomplish,
Rather than pass up on some knowledge.
Get truth you can use,
Walk a mile in dem shoes.

Protect the Troops

Here I am spitting knowledge,
But this ain't no college.
Trying to speak truth,
To these angry and despised youth.

Don't nobody wanna be unique no more?
They trying to get rich by robbing the poor.
Listening to everything put to a beat,
Trying to dance
Instead of moving their feet.

Line them up and take their names,
Make sure they don't stay the same.
Everybody out here is trying to change.

Brother, can you spare a dime?
Please refrain from loose change.
Regroup, think, and redeem the time,
Allow this God to renew your mind.

Would you jump before a smoking gun?
Would you call victory before its won?
Come on, I'm talking to you!
It's time to protect the troops.

Blast Mode

While I'm in this mode,
Figured I'd bid an ode.
Break the silence code,
And rep on blast mode.

Everybody blasting they sound.
They bass boom and shake the ground,
And cancerous lies they spread around.
Well, I'm about to take them down!

Getting ready to turn it up,
Cuz my simple song is not enough.
The Lord saved me!
Time to brag on what He gave me.

Well, my story's always told.
My music's for the souled.
Jesus got ahold.
Now I am on blast mode.

Lord I Lift You Up:

A Hymn

He said if I be lifted up, I'll draw all men
And Father will be gloried, forever
Lord, I praise, I praise.
Lord, I lift You up.
Glorify Your Name.
Lord, I praise, I praise.
You're worthy Oh God.
Mighty is Your Name.

Get Real

Get real, get serious
Make the world delirious
Give the devil fear of us.

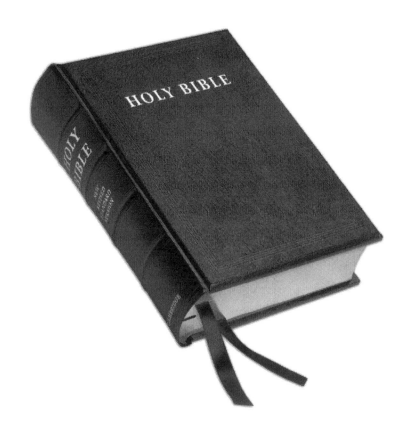

CLOSING THOUGHTS:
EXITING WITH GRACE

In communities where churches and liquor stores share the same space, I hope you have been blessed by this book. My prayer is that God be glorified; that the gifts and talents He has given me be a blessing and motivator to you. May you know where to find hope, no matter where you may be.

To share a hymn:

My hope is built on nothing less
Than Jesus' blood and righteousness
I dare not trust the sweetest frame
But wholly trust in Jesus' Name.

Chorus:

On Christ the solid Rock I stand
All other ground is sinking sand
All other ground is sinking sand.
When darkness seems to hide His face
I rest on His unchanging grace
In every high and stormy gale
My anchor holds within the veil.

(Repeat Chorus).

His oath, His covenant, His blood
Support me in the whelming flood
When all around my soul gives way
He then is all my Hope and Stay.

(Repeat Chorus.)

When He shall come with trumpet sound
Oh may I then in Him be found
Dressed in His righteousness alone
Faultless to stand before the throne.

(Repeat Chorus.)

The Gospel song, "On Christ, The Solid Rock I Stand" is also known as "My Hope Is Built on Nothing Less." This song was written by Edward Mote in 1834.

CALL TO SALVATION:

You may desire hope, faith and love in your life today. We all need hope, faith and love eternally. Ask the Lord Jesus to come into your life. Ask Him to forgive you of your sins and rule in your heart. You may be discouraged and defeated, yet deep in your heart, you are being pulled into the love of God.

Pray "Lord Jesus, come into my life. I admit that I am a sinner. I believe you died and rose again as my substitute. Lord Jesus, make me new. Fill me with your Spirit. Help me to live my life for you and lead me every day. In the Name of Jesus. Thank you."

Amen.

ABOUT THE AUTHOR

Jess Marie (Jessica Marie Smith) has been an avid writer and reader from a young age. She has always seized opportunity to pursue various endeavors with the aid of her family and by the grace of God. She is a graduate of Michigan State University with a Bachelor's degree in Political Science.

She has won recognition from the Famous Poets Society for Outstanding Achievement in Poetry in 2001 at the age of 13. Since she was a child, Jessica has enjoyed sharing short stories, poems and essays with everyone she encounters. Jessica has been featured in various multimedia projects including: the music video *"Heaven Only Knows,"* with Gospel rapper JWill Music, the Trinity Deliverance Church "Soul Explosion," the Millionaires in the Making 2013 cruise, and Examiner.com as a Detroit writer for

Religion and Politics. Jessica has used experience in the multimedia industry in television and radio, along with consulting experience to gain skills and pursue her dreams as an accomplished author. The *Anthology for Hope in the Hood* series is the first published work of many to come.

Jessica is currently a member of The Called and Ready Writers Guild, a Christian-writers support group. The Called and Ready Writers was founded by Minister Mary D. Edwards of Leaves of Gold Consulting, LLC and is currently led by Wanda J. Burnside from Write the Vision Ministries and Media Productions, International. Author Jessica has served numerous positions in church growing up as Membership Clerk, Mime ministry, Choir, Praise Team, Dance and Drama ministry. Currently, she serves the Trinity Deliverance Church performing song in American Sign Language and assisting as a faithful member under the direction of her pastor, Apostle Diane Washington, successor of the late Apostle V.B. Washington.

CONTACT INFORMATION

Jessica Marie Smith
P.O. Box 7113
Novi, MI 48376
Email: jsmithcoinc@gmail.com

You can search *Anthology for Hope in the Hood* on:
Facebook, LinkedIn, Twitter, YouTube

Made in the USA
Columbia, SC
22 July 2024

38583350R00035